IS-906: Workplace Security Awareness

By

Fema

10/31/2013

Course Overview

This course provides guidance to individuals and organizations on how to improve the security in your workplace.

By the end of this course, you will be able to:

- Identify potential risks to workplace security.
- Describe measures for improving workplace security.
- Determine the actions to take in response to a security situation.

Security Begins With You

We live in a world of ever-increasing risk. No workplace – be it a construction site, office building, factory floor, or retail store – is immune from these threats. Risks threaten worker safety, employee morale, and your company's economic livelihood.

Some threats are intentional acts, such as sabotage and violence. Others are caused by natural disasters or manmade accidents. No matter the threat, all employees have a responsibility to help their company protect its employees, information, data, and facilities.

Employees are often the target of these threats as well as the organization's first line of defense against them. Threats endanger the confidentiality, integrity, and security of your workplace, as well as your virtual workplace and computer systems.

As an employee, you are an integral part of your organization's security solution. From the mailroom to the boardroom, security is a shared responsibility. Simply put, security begins with you!

Upon completion, discuss ways you can reduce event exposure and describe specific things you can do to contribute.

Components of Risk

Risk is the potential for an unwanted outcome resulting from an incident, event, or occurrence. The three components of risk to consider are:

- **Threat:** A natural or manmade occurrence, individual, entity, or action that has or indicates the potential to harm life, information, operations, the environment, and/or property.

- **Vulnerability:** Physical features or operational attributes that render an entity open to exploitation or susceptible to a given hazard. Vulnerabilities may be associated with physical factors (e.g., a broken fence), cyber factors (e.g., lack of a firewall), or human factors (e.g., untrained guards).
- **Consequence (Impact):** The effect of an event, incident, or occurrence. For the purposes of the National Infrastructure Protection Plan, consequences are divided into four main categories: public health and safety, economic, psychological, and governance impacts.

Workplace Security

Organizations today employ a number of security measures to reduce risk, such as concrete barriers, obstructions, and gates.

But no matter what type of security measures your organization puts in place, it is important for **ALL** employees to be vigilant for anything unusual at their workplace that could threaten security.

In this course you'll learn that when observing a situation that may threaten security, you should:

- Determine the kinds of behaviors and activities that should be reported.
- Report these activities and behaviors to the appropriate supervisor or security personnel.
- Never confront the situation by yourself.

Please note that the actions described throughout this training are options for you to consider. Whenever possible and applicable, be sure to comply with your company's established policies and procedures.

Understand the Threats

This course presents the following common threats and describes measures you can take in each area to promote a secure workplace:

- Access & Security Control Threats
- Criminal & Terrorist Threats
- Workplace Violence Threats
- Information & Cyber Threats

Access and Security Control Threats

The first threat to the workplace is unauthorized access to sensitive areas or information by persons, equipment, or materials. It is important to secure access points by:

- Limiting the number of access points.
- Using appropriate locks (e.g., padlock, keyed cylinder, or electronic entry control system).
- Controlling doors and other entrances.
- Restricting access to key assets, roofs, and heating, ventilation, and air conditioning (HVAC) systems.
- Using access identification systems such as employee badges, card readers, keypads, and biometric identification.
- Posting signs at access points and restricted access areas.

Access Control Procedures

Typical access control procedures include:

- Identification checks or searches (e.g., employee badge checks, biometrics)
- Procedures to limit who has keys and identification cards and how they can be obtained
- Search or verification procedures for delivery of materials, equipment, or supplies
- Current database of employee-owned vehicles, and protocols for investigating illegally parked cars
- Limited access by contractors, vendors, and temporary employees
- Training for mailroom and receiving personnel in recognizing suspicious items

ID Badges

Many facilities have systems for access control and visitor management deployed throughout the property. These systems grant access to individuals based on their function at the workplace.

Facilities may use ID badges or picture IDs for quick identification of personnel while providing the appropriate level of access control. Many badge types work with proximity readers, allowing individuals to use their badge as a key.

Typical Badge Requirements

If your workplace uses ID badges or other ID security measures, remember that you should:

- Wear your badge on the outermost garment at all times while in the workplace.
- Never allow "piggybacking"—letting an individual follow you through access doors.
- Never lend or borrow badges when an employee has forgotten his or her badge.
- Never allow visitors to share your badge. Only one person should be cleared through an entry point on a given badge.
- Report a lost badge to the appropriate security personnel, manager, or human resources representative immediately.

Sources: Chemical Security Awareness Training/Protect Your Workplace Campaign: Report Suspicious Behavior and Activity Poster

Scenario: Access Controls

It's just past lunchtime, and Kathy is returning to work. On her way in through the employee-only entrance, Kathy spots someone who has his hands full.

Kathy is a helpful person, and she's always very courteous. But something is wrong here.

What should Kathy do differently?

Scenario: Maintaining Access Controls

The person is not using his own pass and is attempting to get Kathy to let him in (i.e., "piggybacking"). She should apologize but pass through the secure employee-only door alone.

To maintain access controls:

- Never allow individuals without appropriate identification into areas where you must use your card or key.
- Don't be confrontational or attempt to restrain the person physically.
- Once inside, immediately contact security or management personnel to explain the situation and describe the individual.

Visitors

Nonemployees should wear a visitor's badge and should be escorted at all times. For more information on the specific security policies for your workplace, please refer to your organization's security officer or management representative.

If your workplace does not use an ID badge system, follow your appropriate recognition methods (for example, vest, hat, or uniform) and apply the recognition procedures and reporting requirements taught in this course.

Unknown Individuals

You should challenge unknown or suspiciously behaving people that you encounter within a secured area if they:

- Are not accompanied by someone you recognize.
- Are not wearing appropriate identification.
- Have an appearance that is inconsistent with the workplace dress code.
- Seem lost or are asking for directions to specific areas.

Note: These standard access security control procedures are based on industry best practices. However, they may not reflect your organization's policy. Please contact your manager or designated security personnel professional for your specific workplace policy on approaching such individuals.

Scenario: Unknown Individual

Anne has a lot on her mind. When she sees a man she does not recognize checking doors down the hall, she hesitates for a split second and then smiles. After all, we all like to be friendly to a new face. The man smiles back as they pass each other.

But Anne missed that something is wrong here. What should Anne do differently?

Scenario: Dealing With Unknown Individuals

The man is not wearing a badge. When you see someone without the employer's proper identification (as per your employer's requirements), you should:

- Approach the person if you are comfortable doing so. Do not approach the person if you feel threatened, and never put yourself in harm's way.
- Notify security personnel or the appropriate manager and provide a description, location, and direction the person is traveling.
- Follow your organization's established policies and procedures regarding surveillance of suspicious or unknown persons.

Challenging Unknown Individuals

If you approach an unknown individual:

- Maintain a safe distance of at least three steps (10 feet) between yourself and the person you are challenging.
- Be persistent in your questioning.
- Do not be easily dismissed. An intruder may give you a brief explanation and just keep on going. (For example: "Sir, may I help you?" "No thanks, I'm fine.")
- Use open-ended questions when addressing a suspected intruder. (For example: "Who are you here to see?" or "What department are you visiting?")
  - A phone call should be made to verify the accuracy of the person's "appointment."
  - Generally, once the conversation starts to get detailed, an unauthorized person will try to evade the situation.
- Notify security or your supervisor.
- If possible, enlist the assistance of a coworker to notify security or your supervisor and assist in keeping an eye on the suspicious person.
- If the individual becomes threatening, abusive, or violent, back off and wait for security and/or your supervisor to arrive.

Criminal and Terrorist Threats

All organizations, from hotels, banks, and grocery stores to manufacturing plants and nonprofit organizations, can be venues for criminal or terrorist activities.

Be alert to any persons who behave suspiciously or engage in unusual actions; these behaviors may be indications of criminal or terrorist activity. Make sure that you:

- Understand how criminals or terrorists could use your facility for their own purposes.
- Promptly alert your security personnel, management, and appropriate authorities when you see suspicious behavior or items, or unusual activity.
- Report something if it looks or feels wrong. Security is everyone's responsibility.

Suspicious Behaviors

It is important to be alert for the following suspicious behaviors:

- Nervous behavior, evasive attitudes, or undue concern with privacy by guests or visitors.
- Attempts to gain access to restricted areas.
- Individuals taking notes, pictures, or videos of facility.

Let's take a look at some scenarios and the recommended actions that should be taken to secure the workplace.

Unusual Events or Suspicious Items

Be alert for:

- Changed or unusual situations around your workplace such as tampered HVAC units, abandoned vehicles, damaged fence line, or missing property.
- Suspicious packages or items, especially:
    - Large amounts of unusual substances (e.g., acetone, peroxide, or drain cleaner).
    - Fumes, odors, or liquids coming from the package.
    - Disassembled electrical components such as wires, circuit boards, or batteries.
    - Plans, drawings, schematics, or maps.

Immediately report the situation to appropriate security or management personnel. Do not go near the area or attempt to open or inspect suspicious items.

Scenario: Suspicious Behaviors

Early one morning, Jill is arriving at work. As she approaches the elevator, she sees a woman up ahead looking up at the security camera. Jill thinks she sees the woman take a picture with a camera phone.

What action should Jill take?

Scenario: Reporting Suspicious Behaviors

Jill should:

- Note the time and place of the incident.
- Report the incident to the appropriate supervisor or security personnel immediately.

When you see someone engaged in suspicious activities such as taking pictures of security cameras or guard posts, you should report it to the appropriate supervisor or security personnel.

However, you should never be confrontational or attempt to restrain the person physically.

Unusual Events or Suspicious Items

Be alert for:

- Changed or unusual situations around your workplace such as tampered HVAC units, abandoned vehicles, damaged fence line, or missing property.
- Suspicious packages or items, especially:
    - Large amounts of unusual substances (e.g., acetone, peroxide, or drain cleaner).
    - Fumes, odors, or liquids coming from the package.
    - Disassembled electrical components such as wires, circuit boards, or batteries.
    - Plans, drawings, schematics, or maps.

Immediately report the situation to appropriate security or management personnel. Do not go near the area or attempt to open or inspect suspicious items.

Scenario: Being Observant

It's Tuesday morning, and it's time to get to work. Kim is telling Joyce about the parent-teacher conference last night.

While they are talking, Joyce notices that the fence has been damaged. What should Joyce do?

Scenario: Acting on Observations

When you see a breach in the security perimeter, such as a hole in a fence, you should immediately notify the appropriate supervisor or security personnel of the problem.

In addition, you should report anything that could compromise the effectiveness of the security measures such as the tree branches near the fence.

Scenario: Suspicious Package

After lunch, Kim and Joyce are walking back to their offices.

Kim notices something unusual. There is an object near the entrance area of their office building.

What action should Kim take?

Scenario: Reporting Suspicious Packages

When you see a suspicious package or item, you should immediately notify the appropriate supervisor or security personnel.

Do not go near the package, and do not attempt to open or inspect the package.

Unattended or Suspicious Vehicles

Organizations today employ a number of security measures (e.g., concrete barriers, obstructions, and gates) to control vehicle and pedestrian access to their facilities. However, security and access control measures can be compromised. For example, vehicles with employee parking permits or decals may be allowed access to certain areas. Security passes can be removed from these vehicles and used on other vehicles, thereby granting unauthorized access to secure areas.

Therefore, all employees must be alert for:

- **Unattended or suspicious vehicles.** Abandoned vehicles may be used to hide suspicious or stolen items, or worse, they could be a vehicle-borne improvised explosive device (VBIED) containing explosives for use in a terrorist act.

- **Changes in vehicle patterns.** Common vehicles such as mail trucks, delivery trucks, buses, or taxis may be suspicious during certain times of day—for example, a second mail delivery, an idle delivery truck, a bus on a different route, or a taxi circling the building numerous times.

Remember, you should:

- Report abandoned vehicles parked on the property or adjacent to your facility.
- Be on the lookout for private vehicles loading or unloading unusual or suspicious items on or around the property.
- Be alert for familiar vehicles arriving at an unusual, unscheduled, or inappropriate time.
- Report your observations to security personnel or an appropriate supervisor immediately.
- Observe and, if possible, write down the vehicle's license plate number and description (make, model, color, body damage, bumper stickers, and accessories).
- Not take any other action except to observe and report the vehicle.
- As a secondary means of reporting, notify local law enforcement.

Source: What's in Store: Ordinary People, Extraordinary Events (Video)

Scenario: Suspicious Vehicle

Sanjay and James are walking back from lunch when James sees a van with no license plates sitting in a no-parking zone in front of the loading dock.

When James steps toward the vehicle for a better look, the person in the driver seat crouches down to avoid James.

Sanjay tells James they'd better keep walking, as they are running late. The men go back into the building without telling anyone about the incident.

What should James and Sanjay do?

Scenario: Reporting Suspicious Vehicles

After James noticed that the van had no license plates, he and Sanjay should have:

- Stayed away from the vehicle.
- Reported the situation to the appropriate security or managerial personnel.
- Noted a description of the vehicle, its location, and the fact that the individual attempted to hide.

Bomb Threat Procedures

If you receive a bomb threat call, take it seriously and use the following procedures:

- Keep calm.
- Keep the caller on the line as long as possible.
- Record every word spoken by the caller on a form such as the sample bomb threat checklist (see next screen).
- Obtain as much information as possible about the caller's threat without antagonizing or threatening the caller.
- Pay particular attention to peculiar background noises and to anything you can glean from the caller's voice, such as gender, accent, and speech pattern.
- Report the incident immediately to the security officer, management representative, and/or your supervisor.

Sources: Department of Homeland Security Bomb Threat Checklist/U.S. Postal Inspection Service Guide to Mail Center Security

Bomb Threat Checklist

Talk to your supervisor or security personnel representative about your organization's bomb threat policy. Bomb threat checklists are extremely valuable and should be made available at all workstations.

If your organization does not have a bomb threat checklist, print the sample for future reference.

Keep a copy of the checklist at your workstation at all times.

Select this link to access the bomb threat checklist.

Suspicious Mail and/or Package

Be alert for:

- Letters that include a threat or have suspicious contents such as white powder or pictures of the workplace.
- Packages with oil or grease spots, an inaccurate address, or excessive postage and/or packaging.

If you encounter a suspicious mail item or package:

- Isolate the item. Do not open or handle it yourself.
- If you do open an item that contains a suspicious substance, evacuate the area and immediately wash your hands with soap and water.
- Contact your management or security personnel.
- Do not destroy written threats or envelopes in which they are received unless directed to do so by your management or security procedures.

Sources: U.S. Postal Inspection Service Guide to Mail Center Security and DHS Best Practices for Safe Mail Handling

Additional Information: Suspicious Mail and/or Package

Bomb Threats in the Mail

If you encounter a written bomb threat, immediately contact your supervisor or security officer, following your organization's security procedures. Written threats provide physical evidence that must be protected from contamination. Do not destroy written threats or envelopes in which they are received unless directed to do so by your management or security procedures.

Suspicious Substances in the Mail

If you open a letter containing a suspicious substance, immediately wash your hands with soap and water. Notify your supervisor or immediately contact your designated security officer. Your security officer may isolate the damaged or suspicious piece of mail or package and cordon off the immediate area. As soon as practical, take a shower with soap and water.

Sources: U.S. Postal Inspection Service Guide to Mail Center Security and DHS Best Practices for Safe Mail Handling

Theft and Diversion

Theft is an unlawful or unauthorized acquisition, by force or stealth:

- By an insider (member of staff).
- By an outsider (someone who is not a member of the staff).

Diversion is an unlawful or unauthorized acquisition, by fraud or deceit.

The type of deception can vary and does not always include failing to compensate the targeted organization.

Scenario: Inventory Irregularities

John and Joyce are passing through the warehouse when John notices one of the containers seems to be missing some of its contents.

This seems odd. The inventory spreadsheet shows that all of the containers are supposed to be full. Joyce is concerned that the container has been tampered with and some of its contents taken.

What action should Joyce take?

Scenario: Reporting Inventory Irregularities

If you discover a container breach, you should immediately report the discrepancy to the appropriate supervisor or security personnel.

Although there may be a reasonable explanation for the discrepancy, shortages should be reported so management can evaluate the situation. Theft can be an indicator of a much larger problem facing security.

Workplace Violence

A current or former employee or an acquaintance of a current or former employee may have the potential to carry out violent behavior at your workplace.

Intuitive managers and coworkers may notice indicators of potentially violent behavior in an employee. In accordance with your organization's policy, alert your manager, security personnel, or human resources department if you believe an employee or coworker exhibits potentially violent behavior.

Source: DHS Active Shooter Booklet

Indicators of Potential Violence

Potentially violent employees typically do not just "snap," but display behavioral indicators over longer periods of time. If these behaviors are recognized, they can often be managed and treated. indicators of potentially violent behavior by an employee may include:

- Increased use of alcohol and/or illegal drugs.
- Unexplained increase in absenteeism; vague physical complaints.
- Noticeable decrease in attention to appearance and hygiene.
- Depression and/or withdrawal.
- Resistance and overreaction to changes in policy and procedures.
- Repeated violations of organizational policies.
- Increased severe mood swings.
- Noticeably unstable, emotional responses.
- Explosive outbursts of anger or rage without provocation.
- Suicidal indications; comments about "putting things in order."
- Behavior that might indicate paranoia ("everybody is against me").
- Increasing discussion of problems at home.
- Escalation of domestic problems into the workplace.
- Talk of severe financial problems.
- Talk of previous incidents of violence.
- Empathy with individuals who commit violence.
- Increase in unsolicited comments about firearms, other dangerous weapons, and violent crimes.

Workplace Violence Resources

Recent active shooter incidents demonstrate the importance of being prepared to respond to workplace violence. The following resources provide additional information on identifying and responding to workplace violence:

- Active Shooter Booklet: This booklet provides guidance to individuals, including managers and employees, who become involved in an active shooter situation, and discusses how to react when law enforcement responds.
- Active Shooter Pocket Guide: This guide provides a brief overview of how best to respond to an active shooter situation.
- Active Shooter Poster: This poster describes how to respond to an active shooter, as well as how to recognize signs of potential workplace violence.

Information and Cyber Threats

Your workplace may use computers to manage day-to-day operations. Organizations control access to computers through computer accounts and passwords. If an unauthorized person obtains the account name and/or password, the security process can fail.

Other types of information or intellectual property, such as copyrights, trademarks, patents, industrial design rights, and trade secrets, may be stored on paper in locked offices or other secure areas. If unauthorized people gain access to those areas by circumventing security protocols, the information may be compromised.

Today, portable electronic devices (e.g., laptop computers, thumb drives, "smart" phones, etc.) have large storage capacity that allows for the storage of thousands of files, which may include sensitive information. For example, a handheld device may contain names, contact lists, company proprietary information, and even passwords. Gaining unauthorized access to these types of devices can severely impact an organization's security.

Scenario: Searching Through Trash

As Betty walks toward the loading dock to wait for a delivery, she notices someone looking into one of the trash bins behind their building.

The man looks around and sees Betty looking at him. He smiles as he quickly turns away from the trash bins.

What should Betty do?

Scenario: Reporting People Searching Through Trash

Betty should note the time and place of the incident and she should report it to the appropriate security or managerial personnel immediately.

The man has no business rummaging through the trash and could be attempting to obtain confidential or sensitive information.

You should always report any such incidents. However, never be confrontational or attempt to physically restrain the person.

Source: Chemical Security Awareness Training

Protecting Information

Organizations need to collect and store information to serve their clients and customers. The more a business knows about its customers, the more able it is to meet their needs.

Clients and customers trust that businesses follow common privacy law principles based on the following Federal laws:

- Privacy Act of 1974
- Freedom of Information Act (FOIA)
- E-Government Act of 2002
- Fair Credit Reporting Act (FCRA)
- Health Insurance Portability and Accountability Act of 1996 (HIPAA)
- Children's Online Privacy Protection Act (COPPA)

Personally Identifiable Information

Personally identifiable information (PII) is any information that permits the identity of an individual to be inferred directly or indirectly. PII includes any information that is linked or linkable to that individual, regardless of whether the individual is a U.S. citizen, a legal permanent resident, or a visitor to the United States. If you collect PII:

- Apply the "need to know" principle before disclosing PII to other personnel.
- Challenge the need for the requested PII before sharing.
- Consider PII materials for official use only.
- Limit the collection of PII for authorized purposes only.

Source: DHS Handbook for Securing Sensitive Personally Identifiable Information

Examples of Personally Identifiable Information (PII)

Name	ZIP code
Social Security number	Account numbers
Date and place of birth	Certificate/license numbers
Biometric identifiers (e.g., fingerprints)	Vehicle identifiers including license plate numbers
Mailing address	Uniform Resource Locators (URLs)
Telephone number	Internet protocol (IP) addresses
Email address	Photographic facial images

Safeguarding Information

To safeguard PII or confidential information:

- Store sensitive information in a room or area that has access control measures to prevent unauthorized access by visitors or members of the public (e.g., locked desk drawers, offices, and file cabinets).
- Never email sensitive information to unauthorized individuals.
- Never leave sensitive information on community printers.
- Take precautions to avoid the loss or theft of computer devices and removable storage media.
- Destroy all sensitive information by appropriate methods (e.g., burn bag or paper shredder) when it is no longer needed.
- Notify your immediate supervisor if you suspect or confirm that a privacy incident has occurred.

Source: DHS Handbook for Securing Sensitive Personally Identifiable Information

Information Security

Just as with physical security, all employees play an integral role in keeping their organization's information from ending up in the wrong hands.

One easy, common sense solution is to adhere to a "clean desk" policy. Here are some simple steps you can take today:

- Put a date and time in your diary or calendar to clear your paperwork.
- Use secure recycling bins for office paper that is no longer needed.
- Do not print emails unnecessarily.
- If possible, handle any piece of paper only once—act on it, file it, or dispose of it.
- Consider scanning paper items and storing them on the hard drive of your computer.
- Always clear your desktop or workspace before you go home.

Source: Safeguarding Sensitive but Unclassified (For Official Use Only) Information

Scenario: Office Visitor and Sensitive Information

Late one morning, Maria stops by and drops a sensitive document onto Pete's desk. Maria asks Pete to make a copy of the entire file. At that moment, a visitor walks up and waits patiently while Maria and Pete are talking. Maria leaves.

A few moments later, the visitor asks Pete if Maria is available to answer a few questions for him. Pete smiles and says that Maria was just here. The visitor asks if he might relay a message to her for him.

Pete offers to catch Maria before she reaches her office. The visitor watches as Pete goes after Maria.

What should Pete have done differently?

Scenario: Retaining Control Over Sensitive Information

The problem is that Pete left the sensitive document unsecured at his desk. He should have stayed at his desk and called Maria.

You should never leave important documents unsecured and unattended. You should properly secure the document, keep it with you, or not leave your desk.

Use of Social Engineering To Obtain Information

Social engineering is one of the simplest, most common, and most successful methods for obtaining information. It is essentially the act of tricking people into revealing personal information, passwords, or other information that can compromise a security system.

Social engineers can be very convincing and can trick or coerce people into revealing information through:

Telephone Interactions

In a telephone social engineering attack, the hacker contacts the victim pretending to be someone else, such as a service technician or fellow employee, and attempts to gather information that may seem innocuous to the victim.

Face-to-Face Interactions

Social engineers may try to collect information about their victims at trade shows or conferences related to the victims' line of work, personal interest, or hobby.

Typically, the social engineer will wander about the event striking up conversations with potential victims. The event gives them a common interest with which to break the ice. They may also go as far as setting up a display or booth to collect information under the pretense of offering a solution or a product related to the event.

Email/Web Interactions

Social engineering can also be conducted in writing via email, postal mail, survey, or other form of written contact with users of a system. Remember:

- Be suspicious of anyone requesting information, especially by phone, Web, or email, and always verify the identity of the person or organization making the request.
- Before entering personal information online, verify that the URL starts with https:// and that you see a closed padlock icon in your browser (often found in the lower right-hand corner of your screen).
- Contact the organization by telephone if there is any doubt as to the authenticity of an email or Web site.
- Contact security if anyone requests your work password(s).

Source: Chemical Security Awareness Training

Example: Social Engineering via Telephone

Attacker: Hi Mark, this is Jean at the Help Desk. How are you doing this afternoon?

Mark: Fine. How can I help you?

Attacker: There was an attempt to hack into the network this weekend. Someone outside the network tried to gain access to several of the user accounts.

Mark: That's not good. Were they able to gain access to our information?

Attacker: We are not sure, so we are running a systems check.

Mark: Okay. What can I do to help?

Attacker: Well, we want to look at your computer log for this weekend to see if there was any unauthorized access or monitoring.

Mark: I was not logged on to the network this past weekend.

Attacker: Great, we can easily obtain the information we need by checking the weekend log. What's your user name?

Mark: My user name is "smithm".

Attacker: And your password?

Mark: My password is "?Golfpro2".

Narrator: Mark just gave his password to an attacker. Remember that no one should ever ask you for your password.

Scenario: Coffee Break

The following scenario depicts an all-too-common social engineering attack.

It is late on Thursday afternoon and George is trying to finish his report before the end of the day. A few of his coworkers come by his desk and invite him to take a break with them for coffee in the cafeteria downstairs.

Luckily, George finds himself at a good stopping point, so it is a perfect time for him to leave his desk for a few minutes. George goes with his coworkers. In a rush, George leaves the document that he was working on open on his computer screen.

What should George have done differently?

Scenario: Avoid Being a Social Engineering Victim

George should not have left his workstation unsecured. It is possible that this may be a situation where social engineering is taking place.

One of his coworkers may have lured George away from his desk in an attempt to allow another individual to gain unauthorized access to his computer. You should always log off or lock your computer, and secure any important papers and personal belongings (e.g., purse, BlackBerry) before leaving your work area.

Lock or log off your computer in accordance with your organization's established procedures.

Source: Chemical Security Awareness Training

Cyber Threats and Vulnerabilities

In the cyber world, a threat is any person, event, or environmental factor that could impact or harm a protected object. A vulnerability is a weakness that can be exploited by a threat: It is the "hole" through which a threat gains access to protected objects or information. Common cyber threats and vulnerabilities include:

Hackers

Hackers attempt to gain unauthorized access to computer networks or systems by intentionally bypassing or compromising their security. Hackers may exploit their illegal access by stealing information or otherwise causing harm to the system or its owners, customers, or users. Examples of possible hackers include:

- Anti-company groups.
- A "kid in the basement."
- A disgruntled employee.
- Industrial or corporate spies.

Cyber Warfare

Cyber warfare is the use of computers and other devices to attack an enemy's information systems as opposed to an enemy's armies or factories.

Malicious Code

Malicious code is any software or program designed to disrupt the normal operation of a computer by allowing an unauthorized process to occur or by granting unauthorized access. Often, the term "virus" is used to refer to all types of malicious code, but malicious code comes in many forms, including:

- Viruses.
- Worms.
- Trojan horses.
- Adware.
- Spyware.

Malicious code threatens three primary security goals:

- **Confidentiality:** Programs like spyware can capture sensitive data while it is being created and pass it on to an outside source.
- **Availability:** Many viruses are designed to modify operating system and program files, leading to computer crashes. Internet worms have spread so widely and so quickly that they have overloaded Internet connections and email systems, leading to effective denial-of-service attacks.
- **Integrity:** Protecting information from unauthorized or inadvertent modification. For example, without integrity, your account information could be changed by someone else.

Note: Malicious code may result in a denial of service. A denial-of-service attack is any cyber attack specifically aimed at disrupting service or blocking access to a particular resource.

Information Gathering

Terrorists and other criminals use cyber tools as part of their information-gathering and espionage activities.

Identity Theft

Identity theft occurs when someone uses your personal identifying information, like your name, Social Security number, or credit card number, without your permission, to commit fraud or other crimes.

Peer-to-Peer Software

Peer-to-peer (P2P) software provides direct access to another computer. Some examples include file sharing, Internet meeting, or chat messaging software. Some P2P programs also have remote-control capabilities. Note: Remote-control software and sites allow users to take control of a computer from another computer somewhere else in the world.

Peer-to-peer software can bypass firewall and antivirus systems by hiding activities of users, such as file transfers. It creates an open channel for malicious code to enter the system. Attackers exploit many of these programs by taking control of an affected computer. Never install unauthorized software on your equipment.

Source: Individual Use and Operation of DHS Information Systems/Computers, DHS Management Directive 4900

Loss of Removable Media

Removable media are any data storage device that you can remove from a computer and take with you. The most common forms of removable media are:

- Compact discs (CDs).
- Portable hard drives.
- USB drives (thumb drives, flash drives, mini drives, micro vaults, memory sticks, and pen drives).

Newer forms of removable media are small and portable and can hold large amounts of data. The storage capacity and small physical size of these devices make them difficult to control. They offer a convenient means of stealing data from or loading data onto another computer.

Passive Threats

Passive threats cause damage without intending to do so. They are unpredictable and difficult to guard against. Even with the best of security systems in place, it is still important to back up information and have disaster recovery plans in place.

Examples of passive threats include:

- Natural hazards.
- Power failures.
- Software glitches.
- Human error.

Cybersecurity Protective Measures

Protective measures to address potential cyber security threats include:

- Firewalls and virus protection systems.
- Password procedures.
- Information encryption software.
- Computer access control systems.
- Computer security staff background checks (at initial hire and periodically).
- Computer security staff training and 24/7 on-call technical support.
- Computer system recovery and restoration plans.
- Intrusion detection systems.
- Redundant and backup systems, and offsite backup data storage.

Strong Passwords

You should never give your password to anyone, and you should create a strong password that:

- Includes a minimum of eight characters with a combination of:
    - Alpha characters in both uppercase and lowercase;
    - Numbers; and
    - Special characters (- ! @ # $ % ^ & * ( ){ } [ ] | + \ - < > ? /) or alternate alpha characters.
- Does not consist solely of a dictionary word in any language, proper noun, name of person/child, pet, or fictional character.
- Does not use information that a hacker could easily obtain or guess about you, such as a Social Security number, serial number, birth date, or telephone number.

Select the following links for additional resources:

- Additional guidance on creating passwords
- Password strength tester

Source: DHS Administrative Policy: DHS Password and User Identification Security

Guidance on Creating Passwords: Do You Use Strong Passwords?

A strong password should appear to be a random string of characters to an attacker. It should be a minimum of eight characters with a combination of alpha characters in both uppercase and lowercase, numbers, special characters (- ! @ # $ % ^ & * ( ){ } [ ] | + \ - < > ? /), or alternate alpha characters.

Alternate Alphabet Characters														
A	@	^	4	**H**	|-|	#	]~[	**O**	0	()	<>	[]	**V**	\/	^
B	3	6	]3	**I**	1	!	|][	**P**	]>	|*	|0		**W**	vv	\/\/ uu
C	<	{	(	**J**	}	_|		**Q**	(,)	0|			**X**	><	%
D	>	|)	)	**K**	|<	]{		**R**	|2	|^			**Y**	\\\|	'/
E	3	(-		**L**	1	|_ #]_		**S**	$	5			**Z**	2	7_
F	Ph	|=		**M**	^^	]v[		**T**	7	+					
G	&	9 6		**N**	/|/	|/|		**U**	|_|	(_)	v				

Here are some good examples, but please do not use these (they are only here as examples):

- Escape!: (eS<@\|>(-!)
- Shopper: ($h<>\|*\|*3R)
- Baddog!: (b@D_\|)<>g!)

NEVER give your password to anyone or lend your account to anyone.

Remember: A password should not consist solely of a dictionary word in any language, proper noun, name of person/child, pet, or fictional character. Also, do not use Social Security numbers, serial numbers, birth dates, telephone numbers, or any information that a hacker could easily obtain or guess about the creator of the password.

Source: DHS Administrative Policy: DHS Password and User Identification Security

Additional Resources

Select the following links to access helpful resources related to workplace security.

- DHS Federal Protective Services Ensuring Building Security Web page provides guidance for handling building emergencies, including suspicious mail, phone threats, bomb or weapon threats, and chemical or biological threats.

- <u>What's in Store: Ordinary People, Extraordinary Events</u> is a video for retail and shopping center employees that provides information to help employees identify and report suspicious activities and threats in a timely manner.
- <u>DHS Bomb Threat Checklist</u> includes bomb threat call procedures and a handy checklist for recording bomb threat information.
- <u>U.S. Postal Inspection Service Guide to Mail Center Security</u> includes guidance for protecting your work site from package bombs, bomb threats, and chemical, biological, and radiological threats.
- <u>DHS Best Practices for Safe Mail Handling</u> identifies best mailroom operations practices used by Federal agencies.
- DHS Active Shooter Materials describe how to respond when an active shooter is in your vicinity. Materials include:
  - <u>Active Shooter Booklet.</u>
  - <u>Active Shooter Pocket Card.</u>
  - <u>Active Shooter Poster.</u>
- <u>DHS Handbook for Safeguarding Sensitive Personally Identifiable Information</u> provides step-by-step guidance on how to identify and protect sensitive PII and simple instructions for encrypting and disposing of sensitive PII.
- <u>Safeguarding Sensitive but Unclassified (For Official Use Only) Information</u> provides DHS policy regarding the identification and safeguarding of sensitive but unclassified information originated within DHS or received by DHS from other government and nongovernmental activities.
- <u>Oregon Department of Human Services: Password and User Identification Security</u> provides guidelines for creating and protecting unique user identifications and "strong" passwords.
- <u>Password Meter</u> is an interactive tool that helps you gauge the strength of your password.

"If You See Something, Say Something™"

DHS launched the "If You See Something, Say Something™" campaign as part of the national Suspicious Activity Reporting initiative. The campaign is a simple and effective program to raise public awareness of indicators of terrorism, crime, and other threats and emphasize the importance of reporting suspicious activity to the proper transportation and law enforcement authorities.

The campaign emphasizes that everyone should:

- Be vigilant.
- Take notice of surroundings.
- Report suspicious items or activities to local authorities immediately.

<u>Select this link for more information about how to report suspicious activity.</u>

The Department of Homeland Security launched a national "If You See Something, Say Something™" public awareness campaign in July 2010. The campaign was originally used by New York's Metropolitan Transportation Authority (MTA), which licensed the use of the trademarked slogan to DHS to help with antiterrorism and anticrime efforts.

Security Is Everyone's Business

Actions taken at the workplace will be dependent upon circumstances. However, you can contribute to your workplace security by:

- Identifying threats and vulnerabilities that affect workplace security.
- Avoiding complacency.
- Observing with all your senses.
- Being aware of unusual changes in your surroundings.
- Noticing unusual or suspicious behavior.
- Knowing whom to call if something is not right.
- Getting assistance. Do NOT try to "handle it" yourself.

Remember, security is everyone's job. Take it seriously.